WE DRIVE Milk Tankers

Ruby Tuesday Books

Alix Wood

Published in 2025 by Ruby Tuesday Books Ltd.

Editors: Ruth Owen & Mark J. Sachner
Design: Alix Wood
Production: John Lingham

Photo credits:
Alamy: 5T (John Eveson), 14 (Taina Sohlman), 15B (Aleksandr Lupin), 16–17 (Michael Doolittle), 18 (Taina Sohlman), 19 (ZUMA Press Inc), 21TR (Mehmet Cetin); iStockPhoto: 1 (halbergman), 6T (halbergman); Shutterstock: 2–3 (CK Foto), 4TL (Clara Bastian), 4TR (New Africa), 4–5B, 6B (KOTOIMAGES), 7T (KOTOIMAGES), 7B (Miguel Perfectti), 8T (Juice Flair), 8B (Ivan Kislitsin), 9BR (Tepepa79), 15T (Kirk Fisher), 21B (Birkir Asgeirsson), 22 (Juice Flair/Olga Popova), 23 (KOTOIMAGES); Shutterstock (Leitenberger Photography): Cover, 9, 10–11, 12–13, 20, 22, 23.

Library of Congress Control Number: 2024949089

Print (Hardback) ISBN 978-1-78856-522-6
Print (Paperback) ISBN 978-1-78856-523-3
ePub ISBN 978-1-78856-524-0

Published in Minneapolis, MN
Printed in the United States

www.rubytuesdaybooks.com

Contents

Where does milk come from?

Milk comes from cows that live on **dairy** farms.

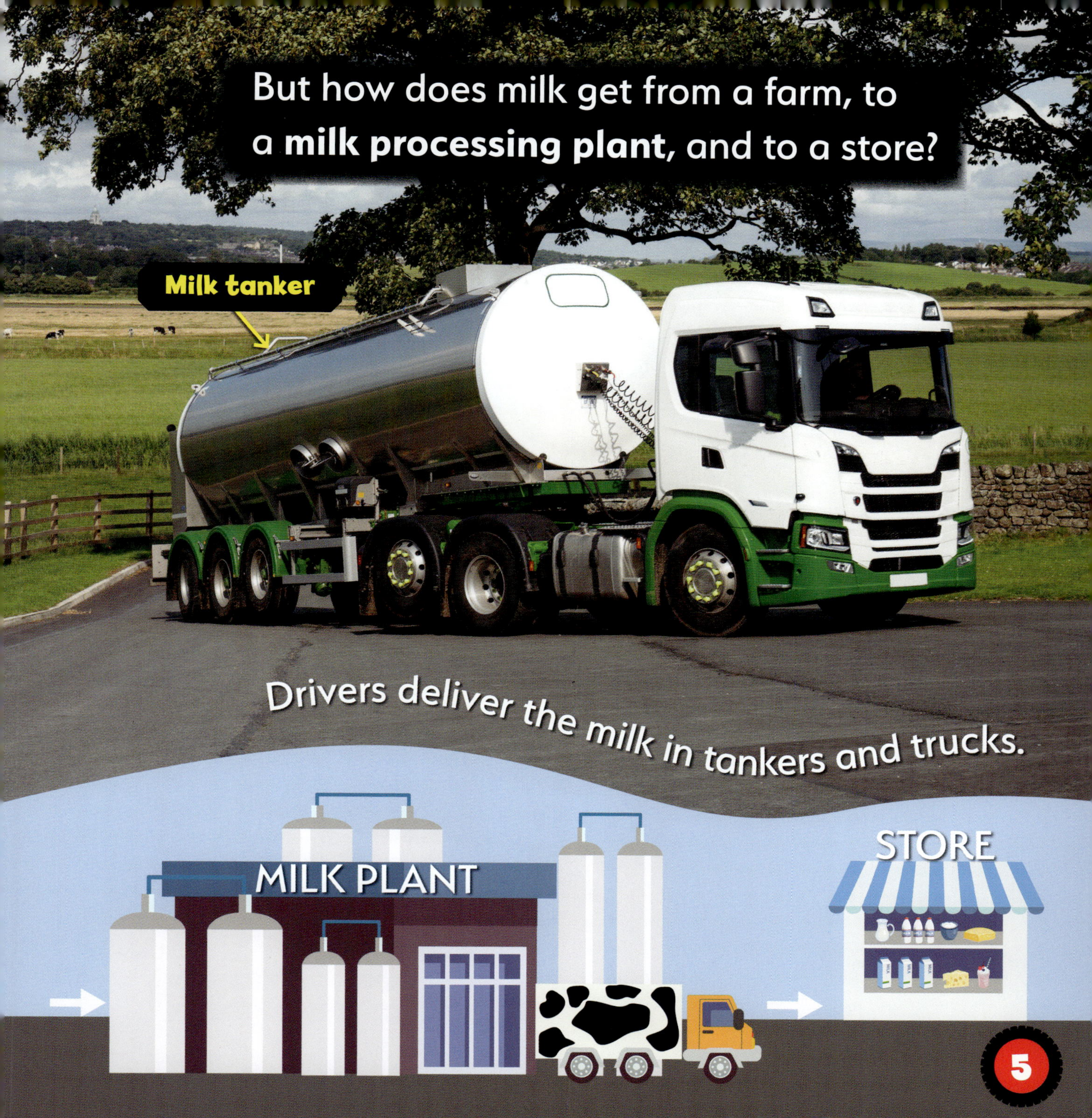
But how does milk get from a farm, to a **milk processing plant**, and to a store?
Milk tanker
Drivers deliver the milk in tankers and trucks.
MILK PLANT
STORE

Milk tanker drivers arrive early at the processing plant.

They check to be sure their tankers are safe to drive.

They fill up with gas.

Checking the air in the tires.

The drivers are told which farms to visit.

Drivers clean their tankers inside and out every day.

Let's go collect some milk!

Tanker drivers collect milk every day of the year.

That's because dairy farmers milk their cows every day—even on holidays.

The fresh milk is stored inside metal tanks in the dairy.

The tanker arrives at the farm.

The cows have been milked and are back in their field.

The farm dog is waiting to say hello!

The tanker driver presses a button to stir the milk in the tank.

He checks a small **sample** of milk.

The sample goes in a cool box on the side of the tanker.

If the milk does not look or smell fresh, the driver will not collect it.

The sample looks good.

The driver pulls the tanker's hose into the dairy.

The driver clips the hose onto the dairy's tank.

The milk pumps from the tank into the tanker.

Some tankers pull a trailer so they can haul even more milk.

Sometimes, a large tanker is too big to fit down a narrow country road.

A small milk tanker

Drivers take a small tanker to collect milk from these farms.

A milk tanker has thick **insulation** to keep the milk cool.

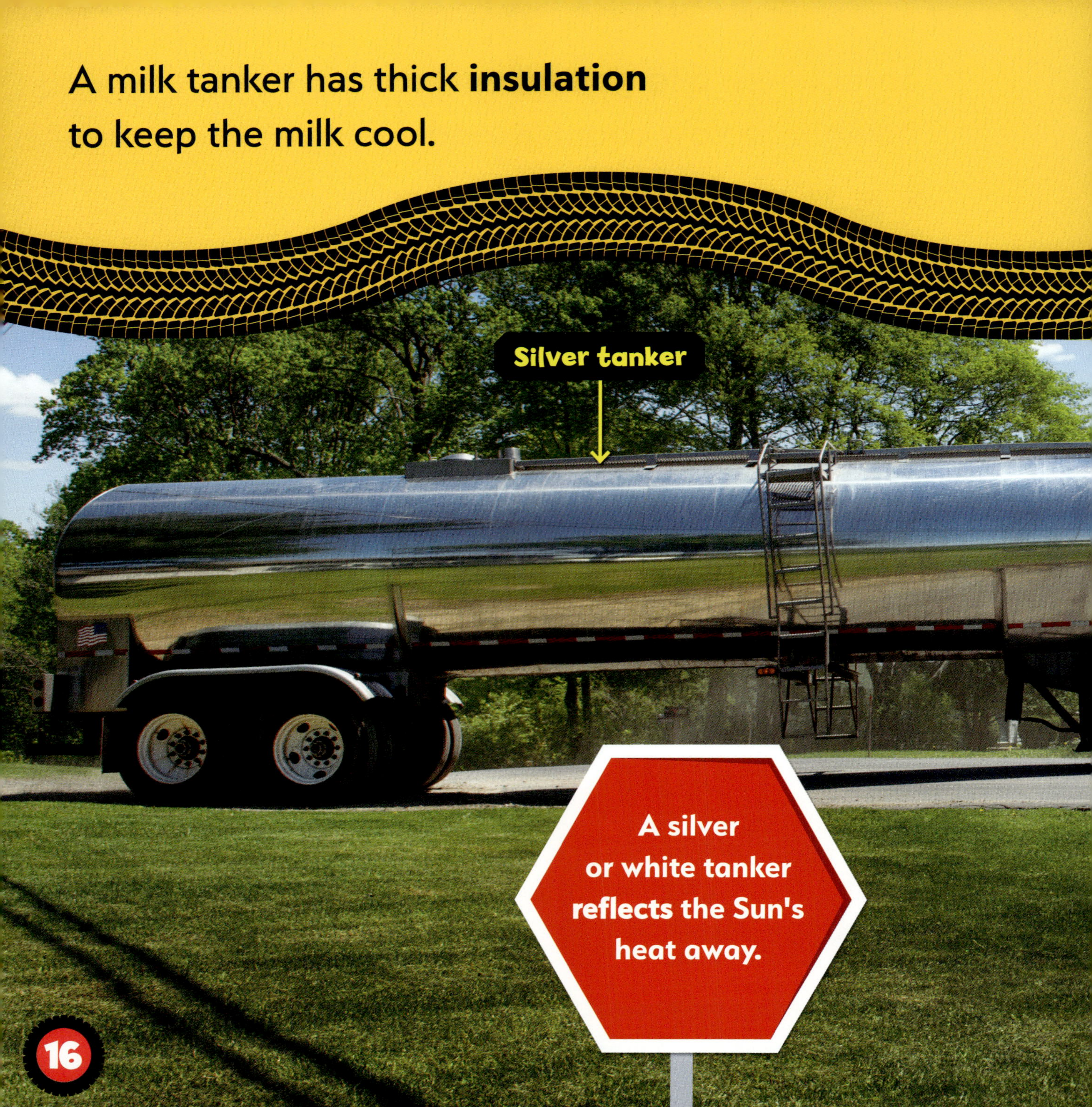

A screen in the cab tells the driver if the milk gets too warm.

The driver can make cold air blow into the tanker.

The driver heads back to the processing plant with a heavy tanker filled with milk.

Milk tanker drivers must deliver their load, whatever the weather.

The milk sloshes from side to side.

The driver must drive very carefully.

Sloshing milk can tip a tanker
if it goes too fast around a bend!

At the plant, a scientist tests the samples to be sure the milk is safe to drink.

The milk pumps from the tanker into big **silos** through hoses and pipes.

Then the driver cleans the tanker.

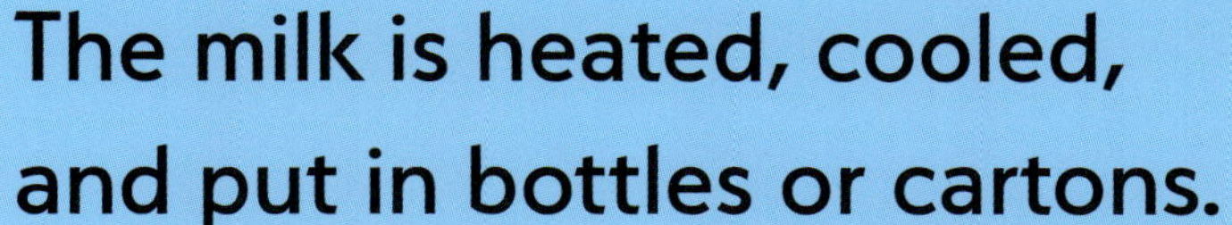

The milk is heated, cooled, and put in bottles or cartons.

A truck delivers the milk to stores.

Back at the farm, the cows are already making more milk.

Tomorrow, the tanker drivers will do it all again!

Glossary

dairy
A building where cows or goats are raised and milked. Also places where milk is stored in tanks or silos.

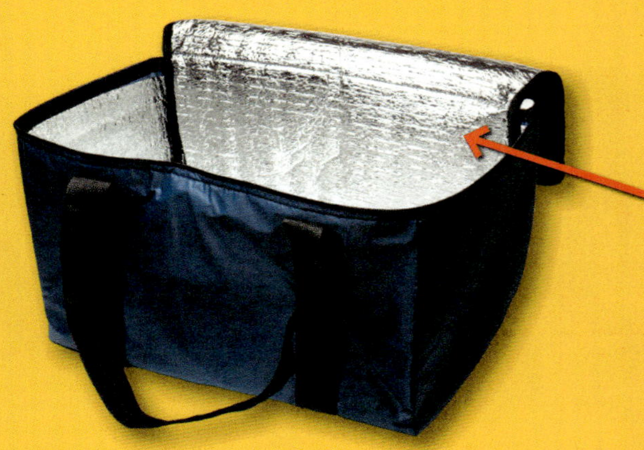

insulation
Materials that help keep things warm or cold.

milk processing plant
A place where milk from farms is put in bottles and cartons. Sometimes the milk is made into cheese, yogurt, and other dairy foods.

reflect
To bounce off something. For example, sunlight that bounces off white or silver surfaces will not make them hot.

sample
A small amount of something that can be checked and tested.

silos
Tall, round towers that store large amounts of food products such as milk or grain.

Index